A Simple, E.
All of Your Hopes, I

...into Reality... Now

By Edgar Maynard

Thought Symbols Press

Thought Symbols
A Simple, Easy to Learn Process Which Will Bring
All of Your Hopes, Dreams and Desires into Reality... Now

Written by Edgar Maynard

Book design by Edgar Maynard

Contents

Page 04
Introduction

Introduction

We've all experienced at least one of the following:

A crazy idea you had for something that became real despite all the odds against it working.

An ambition you thought would never happen that was somehow fulfilled.

That secret dream or wish you had that was inexplicably granted.

Your deepest hope or desire for that something or someone special that just suddenly came into your life exactly as you imagined

All of these things have one thing in common; before they became real they originated as a thought.

Take a second or so and take a look around your surroundings. Is there a television in the room you are in? Can see cars from where you are? Are you wearing nice clothes? Are your favorite books or movies nearby?

The television only exists because someone had an idea for it. Cars only became a reality after someone once imagined replacing the horse. Those nice clothes you are wearing began as someone's ambition to design clothes that people would wear. Your favorite book or movie was created only after someone once thought up a story that they wanted to tell.

Everything man made you have ever seen; every story you have heard or read; every recipe you have ever tried; every TV show or film you have ever watched; every comic book or cartoon character you've heard of; every single brand name you know of; all of these things have

4

the same exact thing in common, they all originated as a thought.

There are people who grew up as kids dreaming of one day travelling into space who are now astronauts. There are people who wanted to own a successful business that are now running corporations that they started from nothing. There are people who just wished to get rich quick and then went out and bought the winning lottery ticket. There are people who had an ambition to lead their country who became the president. There are people who dreamed of finding true love who one day literally bumped into the love of their life and lived happily ever after.

All of those people have the same thing in common. They all had an idea, a dream, an ambition or a hope that became real for them. Or in other words they all once had a thought about something and then that thought turned into reality. A single thought can affect something as simple as what someone will have for dinner that evening to changing the entire world.

Now we come to the reasons why you are reading this book. Why don't most of your own dreams, ambitions or desires ever come true? Why do other people always seem luckier than you? Is there really a way you can change that? Is this book really going to change your life?

Well, I can tell you that there is a way that you can guarantee to bring anything you want into your life *every single time* and everything you need to know is in this book.

This is done by using a process called Thought Symbols.

The amazing thing about Thought Symbols are that you already encounter them on a daily basis and they not only affect your life, they are literally changing the world.

Crazier still is that most people don't even realize they have used Thought Symbols. You have probably at least once in your life inadvertently used a Thought Symbol by accident.

Thought Symbols are so simple and so fantastic that I guarantee that some people who read this book will simply dismiss Thought Symbols as nonsense. In fact there will be people who will read this book, follow the instructions, get the exact thing that they requested and then just dismiss what happened as dumb luck or coincidence.

How can I say this with such certainty? I was one of those people!

When I was first introduced to Thought Symbols I tried it for fun and it worked almost instantly. I then made the mistake of dismissing what had happened as a happy coincidence. However, a few months later I tried using Thought Symbols again on a whim and it worked again. I decided then to take it more seriously and again and again Thought Symbols worked for me. Each time it became harder and harder to dismiss the results I was getting as coincidence until finally I had no option but to accept that Thought Symbols worked no matter how fantastic it sounded or crazy it was.

Anyone can use Thought Symbols and I really do mean anyone. So if you are interested all I ask is that you suspend your disbelief, try Thought Symbols out for yourself and you too will be shocked at the results. After that how you choose to proceed is up to you.

Are you ready to learn? Then let us begin...

*****

Reality has always proved to be much more sophisticated and subtle than any preconceived philosophy.
Michio Kaku

Imagination is everything. It is the preview of life's coming attractions.
Albert Einstein

Chapter One

How to ask for what you want

In this first chapter you will learn how to do something that is probably the most important step in the process of creating and using Thought Symbols. This step is to decide what you want and how to ask for it.

So that you can test out Thought Symbols and see for yourself that Thought Symbols actually do work I want you to think of something small to ask for. You could of course just dive straight off the deep end and use Thought Symbols to get something life changing that you have always wanted immediately, but I would suggest starting out small. There's no rush and you would be best to ask for the big things once you get used to Thought Symbols and have tried using them a few times. There are two reasons I would ask for that you do this:

1) If you don't ask for what you want correctly it is possible to get unexpected and unwanted results (I'll explain this later on)

2) By requesting something small you won't get too freaked out when what you requested suddenly appears or occurs!

So as a complete beginner I ask you please to think of something small for your very first attempt at using Thought Symbols. If you're having difficulty thinking of something small here are some suggestions of the sort of request you could make:

To find a quarter (or a similar coin if you live outside the USA)

To have unexpected contact with a friend

To see someone wearing a specific item of clothing (e.g. to see a woman in a green dress or someone wearing bright red shoes)

To hear one of your favorite songs

To receive a compliment from a stranger

Do you get the idea? So either use one of the above suggestions or come up with one of your own.

Before you turn your request into a Thought Symbol you first have to make sure that you word your request properly. This means that you must turn your request into as simple and as straightforward a statement as possible. To show you what I mean I shall use the example "to find a quarter".

So how should you ask "to find a quarter"? If you thought the answer was to ask "I want to find a quarter" or "I wish I could find a quarter" then I'm afraid you are incorrect. If you "want" or "wish" for something then chances are it will never happen. This is because if you use the words "want" or "wish" when you word your request then all you are saying is that you desire something. So unless your intention is for that something you want to remain just a dream or a desire then "want" or "wish" are words you should not use.

What you should be doing is wording your request for whatever it is that you want as a statement of intent. This means that you should avoid using the words "I want" or "I wish" and instead word your request "I will" or "I shall".

So still using the example "to find a quarter" I would word this request as the statement "I will find a quarter". It is the request "I will find a quarter" which will then become my Thought Symbol.

I cannot stress the importance of wording your request properly. This is because whatever you request will happen just as you have asked. So if your request was worded "I want to find a quarter" then that is exactly what will happen; you will find yourself for a while after using the Thought Symbol wanting to find a quarter. In fact you might for a short while find yourself obsessing over coming across a quarter!

If however you simply state your request as "I will find a quarter" then sure enough, after using the Thought Symbol that is exactly what will happen; you will find a quarter.

Please keep this in mind especially when you start to use Thought Symbols to ask for bigger or life changing things to occur or to appear in your life. When you use a Thought Symbol for that sort of request it is even more important for your request to be carefully worded.

Take the example of the quarter. If you ask for something small like a quarter it really needs no explanation as to why a quarter would just suddenly appear from nowhere into your possession. A quarter is too inconsequential to disrupt or affect your life by suddenly appearing. So it does not matter if you just ask "I will find a quarter" without being any more detailed than that.

If however, you ask for a larger sum of money like $500 then unless you also specify a reason or a way for that money to appear then although the $500 will still appear as you have asked there is a chance that it might manifest itself into your life in an undesirable way.

The warning story I was told by the person who first introduced me to Thought Symbols was about someone who did exactly that. They used the request "I shall receive $500" for their Thought Symbol. Shortly after using their Thought Symbol they wrote off their car in a traffic accident and a week or so after the accident they received the amount of $500 into their bank account from their car insurance company. They got the $500 that they wanted but by being too simplistic and just asking for $500 instead of also specifying how the $500 might appear they also got unexpected and undesirable side effects.

What that person should have done was to also specify how they wanted their request to appear. So if for instance they had used the request "I will win $500 in a game of chance" for their Thought Symbol then all they would have to do afterwards is buy a few lottery tickets or enter some competitions with a $500 cash prize. After using their Thought Symbol they would have won the $500.

If they had only just taken the time to think of and then specify a way for the $500 they wanted to appear then they would have avoided their request manifesting into their life in a random manner such as a car crash.

Using Thought Symbols to find love, friendship or even to change an existing relationship is possible but requires careful thought into how you word your request. Thought Symbols will definitely bring people into your life, help change the dynamics of an existing relationship or affect how people initially perceive you but because everyone has free will you would not be able to use Thought Symbols to make people do things against their will.

You could for instance use Thought Symbols to bring a beautiful woman or handsome man into your life but you could not make them love you. Because of free will that decision would be theirs to make.

A male friend used a Thought Symbol in order to meet lots of good looking blonde women purely because he quite liked the idea of being in a relationship with a gorgeous blonde woman. His request was "I will have many beautiful blonde women enter my life". Sure enough for several months he had many attractive blonde women enter his life. However, he later related to me that although he had got exactly what he had asked for the universe had taken his request too literally.

My friend had wanted to meet a beautiful blonde woman he could possibly have a relationship with but because he had not specified this in his request he instead just got what he had requested; a succession of beautiful blonde woman entering his life. The problem was that hardly any of them were even attracted to him let alone the sort of person he would want to be in a relationship with. The end result was that he was just as lonely as he had been previously. This was because he had used Thought Symbols incorrectly.

I explained this to my friend and so to remedy his situation he used another Thought Symbol to stop all the blonde women randomly manifesting into his life. A few weeks later he used another Thought Symbol, this time making a more detailed request stipulating that he would meet a woman he would be compatible with and that they would be mutually attracted to each other. Sure enough, shortly after using this Thought Symbol he found himself in the company of a woman who just a few months after their first encounter moved in with him. The following year they were married and more recently they had their first child.

Thought Symbols can also be used to request that people perceive or treat you in a certain way. This does work, although in my experience usually only for short interactions or initial meetings with others that you would like to go in a certain way. However, you have to be specific with your request and every time I have tried this type of Thought Symbol I find that the effect only lasts until the other person gets to know you properly after which their free will takes over.

An example of this that I have used myself would be the time I used a Thought Symbol for a job interview. At that time I had been passed over for promotion twice in the job I was working in. Then a year later, not long after I had discovered Thought Symbols, I had a third chance of promotion. I used a Thought Symbol to ask that the people interviewing me would think I was a perfect candidate for the promotion. For the time leading up to the interview I found myself putting extra effort into my preparation and when it came to the interview it could not have went any better.

Although I was told at the end of the interview that it would be a few weeks before I would find out if I had been successful I walked out of that room knowing I had got that promotion. Sure enough when I came home from a family holiday a few weeks later the letter offering me a promotion was waiting for me.

Another way of using Thought Symbols (which we'll touch on near the end of this book) is when you want something that will require lots of people for it to be successful or are doing something that would work better if it involved lots of people. Examples of this would be having people listen to your song, having people come to your party, starting a new craze or selling a product.

Almost all of the best known brands such as soft drinks, movie franchises and even the biggest bands in music all use Thought Symbols in this way. I cannot say if they are doing so intentionally or unintentionally but they are using a form of Thought Symbols nonetheless and I will explain how you too can do this later in the book.

Now that I have explained the importance of asking for what you want correctly and why for your first attempt you should ask for something small I want you to stop and decide what small thing you are going to ask for. To demonstrate the Thought Symbol process to you I will use my example "I will find a quarter" from earlier.

If you join me in Chapter Two I will show you how to create a Thought Symbol using your request..

*****

Chapter Two

Turning your request into a Thought Symbol

So what exactly is a Thought Symbol? A Thought Symbol is the image that you create from your carefully worded request. This Thought Symbol is then used to bring your request into your life.

How you will use the Thought Symbol to bring your request into your life I will show you in the next chapter. Before I can do that you must first learn how to create a Thought Symbol.

Unlike the previous stage in the process there is no need to be exact or careful. As long as you start with a carefully worded request there is no right or wrong way to create a Thought Symbol. So, if after reading this book you want to come up with your own method of creating your Thought Symbols then go ahead. However for your very first attempt at creating a Thought Symbol I would suggest using the simple method I will show you in this chapter.

So as an example I will use the simple request "I will find a quarter" from the previous chapter and show you in four easy steps how to create a Thought Symbol from this request.

So how do you create a Thought Symbol? You start by simply writing your carefully worded request down on a sheet of paper.

Step One

Write down your carefully worded request on a sheet of paper. In this example we will write down "I will find a quarter" (see Example 1).

Example one

I WILL FIND A QUARTER

Step Two

Next, you will remove all the vowels from your request. This changes the request "I will find a quarter" to "wll fnd qrtr" (see Example 2).

Example two

I WILL FIND A QUARTER

WLL FND QRTR

Step Three

Next you will remove any duplicated consonants. This further changes the request from "wll fnd qrtr" to "wl fnd qrt" (see Example 3).

Example three

I WILL FIND A QUARTER

WLL FND QRTR

WLFNDQRT

Step Four

This is the fun bit. You will use the string of remaining letters to create a unique symbol. You can spend as much or as little time on this stage as you want. The end result of this process is your own unique symbol.

As you will see from my example I have gradually created a totally unique symbol just by using the remaining letters and a little bit of creativity. I started off with the string of letters. I then made a crude image using all of the letters. I then redrew the image, starting to get a little artistic. Finally, I redrew the image one last time, turning it into my finished image (see Example four)

Example four

1) Start with the remaining letters   WL FND QRT

2) Combine the letters together

3) Start to get artistic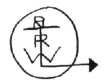

4) Keep going until you're done

Although I have shown you an example of a fully completed symbol please remember that when you create your own symbol that it can look any way you want it to look. The important part is that as long as the symbol you create starts off as your carefully worded request and uses those letters as a starting point you can go as crazy as you want.

So when you get to step four do what you want. You can combine letters together, add lines to the image, remove lines, add shapes, add colors, add shading, there is literally no limit to what you can do. If you want your symbol to finish up looking like a brand logo then that is fine. If you want your symbol to look like a tribal motif then do it. If you want your symbol to look as if it's a magical symbol then go ahead.

As long as you always start off with your carefully worded request, how the symbol winds up looking at the end is entirely up to you. Even the medium or materials you use to create your symbol are entirely up to you. You can if you wish just do as I have shown in this book and use a pen and paper to create your symbol. But if you are artistic or are feeling creative and want to use paint, chalk, colored pencils, crayons or even a tablet or computer to create your symbol then you should do exactly that.

Also don't worry if you don't have an artistic bone in your body. If your images always wind up looking like a toddler has gone crazy on a bit of paper it honestly doesn't matter. As long as you always start off with your carefully worded request it will work.

Once you have created your very own symbol then congratulations are in order as you have just completed the hardest part of the process and this unique symbol is your Thought Symbol!

Now that you have your Thought Symbol prepared you just need to know how to make your Thought Symbol work. What you will do in the next part of the process to make your Thought Symbol you might find a bit strange or even ridiculous (I know I did). However it is a quick, easy and simple process to carry out and afterwards you won't have to do anything else except wait for your request to appear.

If you join me in Chapter Three I will show you exactly how you do this and if you then try it out for yourself you will soon have your very own Thought Symbol realize whatever it is you have requested into your life.

*****

Chapter Three

Activate & Send / Eradicate & Dismiss

This chapter covers the last part of the process where you have to do anything. After you complete this part of the process you can sit back, relax and wait for whatever you have requested to manifest itself into your life.

In the example I have been using in this book I have shown how I would create a Thought Symbol so that I will find a quarter. What my Thought Symbol will do for me if I complete this last part of the process is send out my request to the universe to manifest a quarter for me to find. Once I have done this I can be assured that after a short period of time I will find a quarter.

In order for this to work all you have to do is simply follow the directions for this final part of the process and your Thought Symbol will do the rest. The final part of the process involves doing four simple actions which are performed over two stages:

Stage One is where you Activate & Send your Thought Symbol.

Stage Two is where you Eradicate & Dismiss your Thought Symbol.

You may feel silly doing this last part of the process the first time you attempt it and will probably have doubts that this will even work for you. It sounds so far fetched that I know I did. All I can do is assure you that any doubts you may have will start to be dispelled when your first request suddenly appears just as you asked. You might be spooked by this or perhaps even try and dismiss it as a coincidence but as soon as your first Thought Symbol works exactly as you requested I urge you to try it again.

Stage One Activate & Send

Activating and sending your Thought Symbol is something that can only be performed when your conscious mind is in an altered state allowing your subconscious mind to take over. This means that you must be experiencing one or more of the following states of mind; empty of almost all thought; being distracted suddenly; being in a state of confusion; being in a state of euphoria; being startled; being mentally exhausted; or being in a trance like state.

So basically, as long as you are experiencing any altered state of mind where your conscious mind has momentarily switched off you are at that moment ready to activate your Thought Symbol. It is whilst you are in this brief moment of altered state of mind that you can activate your Thought Symbol, turning it from a simple sketch on a piece of paper to a powerful request that you have sent out with your mind for the universe to fulfill.

If you practice meditation or yoga then you will already be familiar with the sort of mental state I am talking about and you are more than welcome to use either of those methods to achieve this mental state.

For everyone else, don't worry! This may sound terribly complicated but it's actually very, very simple. You don't have to learn how to meditate or yoga to make this work. There are very quick and very easy ways which will allow you to achieve this state of mind. Also, it is only necessary to achieve this altered mental state for a very brief moment of time in order to activate and send your Thought Symbol. In fact such a brief a moment of time is required that you literally need barely a second or so of being in this altered mental state

So, to show you that you do in fact know what I am talking about and that you have in fact already experienced these states of mind countless times before, I will give you some everyday examples. I'm talking about those few seconds just after you wake up in the morning or just as you fall asleep at night; that instant just after someone gives you a fright; those times when you're driving then it suddenly occurs to you that you have switched off and have been driving on auto-pilot; that moment when you were on a rollercoaster and went over that first drop; that time you were bored in class, zoned out and then the teacher called out your name; those occasions when you were dancing to or listening to a piece of music so intensely that you almost forgot where you were; and finally, the moment when you experience an orgasm.

It is when you are experiencing the sort of brief, altered mental state as described above that you activate and send your Thought Symbol.

This is done by simply gazing upon the Thought Symbol that you created, and as soon as you feel this altered conscious state start to subside (which will be almost immediately) you close your eyes and visualize your Thought Symbol. You then visualize the image of your Thought Symbol becoming brighter and brighter before you finally send this mental image of your Thought Symbol quickly away from you like a shooting star flying off into the cosmos.

To achieve this altered state of mind is really simple and there are almost endless ways to achieve it. You will probably come up with your own alternative methods in time but to start you off here are some suggestions for you to try out:

Sit in a darkened room with a candle and stare at the dark centre of the flame, concentrating on nothing except that dark centre. Do this until your mind empties and your vision closes in around you.

Put on music, start dancing and keep dancing until you are completely lost in the moment. Very rhythmic, dance music is best for this.

Tune your radio into static, close your eyes and concentrate on the sound of the static until your mind is empty.

Play a racing game on a computer games console and drive until you are completely lost in the game and are driving on auto-pilot.

Stare at yourself in a mirror until you lose all sense of yourself and it feels that you are absent mindedly staring at a stranger.

Finally, the easiest method of all for beginners... bring yourself to an orgasm (this is not only the easiest method it is also the most reliable method for beginners to use as it works every single time).

And just to repeat those directions, once you are in your altered mind state you will:

Gaze at your Thought Symbol

As your altered mind state starts to subside (which will be almost immediately) close your eyes

Keep the image of your Thought Symbol in your mind's eye and visualize the Thought Symbol getting brighter and brighter

Finally visualize sending your Thought Symbol flying away from you out to the distant universe

Once you have done this your Thought Symbol is now out there and beginning to work on your behalf to bring your request into your life. But to finish the process properly you now have to eradicate and dismiss your Thought Symbol.

*

Stage Two Eradicate & Dismiss

This is the last stage in the process and perhaps the easiest part of all. First you must eradicate the Thought Symbol you used. This means that if your Thought Symbol was on a piece of paper then simply destroy the piece of paper. Burn it, tear it into pieces, eat it, do whatever you want, as long as the Thought Symbol you used is completely destroyed. If you made your Thought Symbol on a whiteboard with a dry marker pen or on a blackboard with chalk then simply wipe your Thought Symbol away. If you painted your Thought Symbol onto your hand then wash it off. If your Thought Symbol is an image on your computer or tablet then delete the file. You get the idea.

As soon as you have eradicated your Thought Symbol you now have to dismiss your Thought Symbol from your mind. The simplest and best way to achieve this is to just go and do something else. Go and have a meal, read a book, watch a film, go to the gym, play a game, phone a friend. Do anything else at all in order to remove the Thought Symbol from your mind and stop yourself from dwelling upon it.

You don't have to forget all about your Thought Symbol as that would be almost impossible to achieve. It is perfectly fine and normal to occasionally think about your request. Your Thought Symbol will work as long as you are not constantly wondering when your request is going to appear or actively waiting for your request to come into your life.

The reason for eradicating and then dismissing your Thought Symbol is because in order for the Thought Symbol to work you must first release it from your mind, allowing your request to be fulfilled by the universe. If instead you hold onto your Thought Symbol, keep returning to it, thinking about it, and dwelling upon it then it will either take a long, long time to appear or it will not appear at all. I'll explain why this is so in the next chapter (and in the chapter after that I will teach you about another type of Thought Symbol where you don't eradicate your Thought Symbol at all).

*

So to summarize, using the example of requesting "I will find a quarter", I would activate and send my Thought Symbol using one of the methods described. Then I would destroy piece of paper with the Thought Symbol on it. After this I would tidy up and then perhaps go for a nice meal with a friend putting all thoughts of my request from the forefront of my mind. What will then happen next is I will be doing something completely ordinary, such as walking down the street a day or so later, when suddenly I will find a quarter. I will experience the same thrill I always get at realizing that one of my Thought Symbol requests has just been delivered to me by the universe. Then I will pick up the quarter I just found and put it in my pocket.

In the next chapter I will discuss the bit just before I found the quarter; the wait.

*****

Chapter Four

The wait

How long will my Thought Symbol take to work? When is my request going to arrive? This is the part of the process you have absolutely no control over. The wait.

All I can tell you is that it will take as long as it takes. If you are asking for something small then in my own personal experience the longest time that elapsed before a small request was granted was about a week. For bigger things this wait can take longer as your request will always manifest itself in such a way that could also be dismissed as coincidence or dumb luck.

What will definitely make the wait longer is to keep thinking about your request constantly after you have made it. In my experience just about every request I've made has been granted after I had almost forgotten about my request or had just not thought about it at all.

My theory as to why this happens is that if you are constantly thinking about your request then this somehow prevents your request from being fulfilled. I believe that this may have something to do with the fact that whatever your request is originally started off as a desire.

When you use this process you are converting a desire for something into a Thought Symbol. This Thought Symbol is then activated and sent out as a request for the universe to fulfill. If however, after activating and sending your Thought Symbol, you do not put your request to the back of your mind and instead continue to cling on to the desire by constantly think about it this means it will remain just that; an unfulfilled desire.

To prevent this from happening you can use a technique that I myself usually use. What I do to make the "eradicate and dismiss" part of the Thought Symbol process easier for myself is to create several Thought Symbols for several different requests at once. However, instead of completing the last two stages of the process I stop and put the Thought Symbols away.

I do this by gathering up all the Thought Symbols I created, mix them all up and then I put them away in a drawer or in my wallet for a few days (or sometimes a lot longer). Then at a later time I will take out one of these previously prepared Thought Symbols at random and complete the last two stages of the process (Activate & Send / Eradicate & Dismiss). I guarantee that you will find these last steps a lot easier to complete as you may not know which Thought Symbol is which or indeed even remember what it was you created the Thought Symbol for in the first place.

Doing the above won't be necessary on your first attempt at the Thought Symbol process. This is because you will be asking for something small and inconsequential that you don't really care about and also because you will most likely be trying the process out of curiosity, not really believing that Thought Symbols work.

As soon as that first request is granted though you should immediately try it out again. Do not repeat the same mistake I made when my first request was suddenly granted after a few days (my first success was the day after I had decided that Thought Symbols were nonsense). The mistake I made was that although the process had worked I dismissed it as a coincidence and I left it at that. It was months later before I tried it again on a whim for fun and realized soon afterwards that it actually did work.

I mentioned previously that there is a different method of doing this process that does not involve destroying your Thought Symbol and also involves other people. If you go to the next and final chapter I'll briefly give examples of this and explain some ways you can do this yourself.

*****

Chapter Five

Other Thought Symbols

This final chapter briefly covers other types of Thought Symbols. What will surprise you is that you will already be familiar with some of these. However, as I have only ever encountered two other people to have learned about Thought Symbols independently of me (and one of them was the person who taught me) I would wager that the majority of the following examples of other Thought Symbols have been created by accident (although I wouldn't be surprised if some of the examples I am about to mention did know that they were creating a Thought Symbol but have kept this process a secret).

Think of your favorite brand names. What do they all have in common? A brand logo. Every brand logo you've ever seen is a Thought Symbol. The creation of a brand logo is almost identical to the method you use when creating your own Thought Symbols.

The difference is that in order for a brand logo to work effectively it requires many people to subconsciously activate and send it. However, because these people are not involved in the creation process; are not aware that they are even doing anything; and the more people that see the Thought Symbol the better; then obviously the person creating this type of Thought Symbol would not destroy it, in fact they would more likely duplicate it and have it in as many places as possible for as long as possible. As for dismissing the Thought Symbol, again there is no need for the person creating the Thought Symbol to dismiss it as they would not be activating or sending the Thought Symbol.

So if you are ever creating a logo for a product you want to sell or for something else, such as for a band you are in that you want to be successful, you are in fact creating a type of Thought Symbol.

If you are creating a logo for this purpose then you now know that all you have to do is keep the purpose behind that logo in your mind as your create it then your logo will also be a Thought Symbol. If you do this then after your logo is complete all you have to do is put it out there and let anyone who sees it subconsciously activate it for you. It will then work as you desire.

There are other similar Thought Symbols which demonstrate how powerful Thought Symbols can be and how long people have been using them for...

What does every country have in common? A flag. A flag is a type of Thought Symbol that is created for an entire country.

Think of all the world's major religions. They all use Thought Symbols. The Christian Cross, the Judaism Star, the Islamic Crescent & Star are all Thought Symbols.

Signs of the Zodiac? Those are Thought Symbols that influence how people behave depending on what time of year they were born on.

Even political parties use Thought Symbols. The best example I can think of this (and also the worst); the Nazi Swastika.

As you can see because some of these Thought Symbols have many, many people constantly repeating the request they can take on a life of their own, far exceeding even the wildest ambitions of their creators. Because the most successful of these Thought Symbols are used by so many people they have become so powerful that even though they may just be an image of abstract shapes or colors just by looking at some of them will make you think of what they stand for or even make you feel or act in a certain way.

So if you want to use a Thought Symbol to get lots of people to do something that you want or just because you want to do something big that would work better or be more successful if it used lots of people to activate it then you should consider using Thought Symbols in this way to achieve your goal.

You can even use Thought Symbols in a subtle, less obvious or "hidden" way so that people are completely unaware that they are even being shown a Thought Symbol that they will then activate.

Examples of this that I've used myself are to change my avatar on websites and social media to a Thought

Symbol I've created. Sometimes my Thought Symbol will just be a small addition to an existing picture such as putting it in the corner of a photo.

I know of people who have created posters, flyers, buttons and stickers with a Thought Symbol on it which they then placed or left in all sorts of random places where they would be seen by many people. They all used this type of Thought Symbol because they were each involved in a project that they wanted to be successful. The projects were a club night, a theatre production and a friend's band. All three experienced great success with their ventures and all three of them acknowledge at least partial credit to their success to the Thought Symbols they used.

You could even have a Thought Symbol on your rucksack, on a mug or on a t-shirt in order to have people who see you with the Thought Symbol repeatedly activate and send it for you. This is especially useful if you have a request that you wish to be ongoing. I even know of someone who had their Thought Symbol (which was to bring them good fortune) tattooed onto themselves. A bit extreme I know but she is possibly the luckiest person I know!

Finally, to demonstrate to you that this type of Thought Symbol works, I created and placed a Thought Symbol on the cover and inside this very book. The fact that you are reading this book I hope shows you that this has worked.

*****

Afterword

So now know how to create Thought Symbols and what to do to make them work.

If you have read to this point then you are almost certainly at least curious to try this out and see if Thought Symbols work. All I can do is assure you that as long as you follow the instructions I have laid out in this book your Thought Symbols will always work for you.

Ever since I first started using Thought Symbols I have been spreading the word so that others can experience what I have experienced. In fact I have taught Thought Symbols to so many others that a friend jokingly suggested I should perhaps write it all out as a short instructional book. This is that book.

I mentioned in the introduction that you have probably at least once in your life already used Thought Symbols without realizing it. Most of us have at some point sat down with a pen and paper and perhaps absent mindedly made a doodle whilst day dreaming about something we desired. If you can recall doing that and also recall by coincidence the thing you desired then coming into your life then you inadvertently created and used a Thought Symbol. The difference now is that you now know how to create and use Thought Symbols properly so that you can always get what you want every single time.

Whenever I teach Thought Symbols to someone new I am usually asked the same question which you are probably also wondering; How do Thought Symbols work? The honest answer is that I do not know. I do however have a theory.

I like to preface my theory with this; the universe created us and we then evolved to a point where we became so intelligent that we developed spoken languages as a way for us to communicate ideas to each other. We then further evolved our spoken languages into symbols that became our written languages. It is this evolution of communication and written language that has allowed us to share and pass knowledge on to each other. Over time it is this combination of our thoughts and our written language that have allowed us to change and manipulate our entire world.

So my theory is this; Thought Symbols are perhaps a higher form of language, above our spoken and written languages.

To explain, I imagine that Thought Symbols are working with the universe in a similar fashion to instructions given to a computer by a programmer. A programmer uses computer code that they then input to the computer with a keyboard in order to produce whatever they want on a computer screen. As you can see unless you know how to convert your instructions into computer code or that you have to communicate your instructions to the computer using the keyboard then the computer is never going to work for you and do what you want.

So to me Thought Symbols are just another form of language and the process shown in this book is how you communicate that language directly to the universe. By communicating our desires and requests to the universe in this manner then just like a computer the universe just does as it is commanded to.

That may sound crazy but consider this; when you read this book I am directly communicating with you inside your head from the time when I wrote this book. If that is the power of our basic written language then how powerful are Thought Symbols?

It's just a theory but I'm sure it's something you will also ponder upon once you see Thought Symbols working for you.

Before you leave my final advice for you is this; have fun with your Thought Symbols, use your Thought Symbols carefully and use your Thought Symbols for good. If you use your Thought Symbols correctly you can and will change your life for the better. Your hopes, dreams and desires really are about to become reality!

*

Made in the USA
Middletown, DE
02 August 2015